·VISUAL GUIDES·

SPACE MACHINES

·VISUAL GUIDES·

SPACE MACHINES

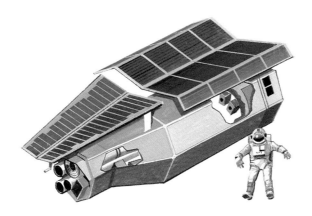

Norman Barrett

FRANKLIN WATTS

New York • Chicago • London • Toronto • Sydney

© 1994 Franklin Watts

Franklin Watts
95 Madison Avenue
New York, NY 10016

Library of Congress
Cataloging-in-Publication Data
Barrett, Norman S.
    Space machines / Norman
    Barrett.
       p. cm. – (Visual guides)
    Includes index.
    ISBN 0-531-14300-7
    1. Space vehicles – Juvenile
    literature.   [1. Space
    vehicles.]
    I. Title.   II. Series: Barrett,
Norman S.   Visual guides.
TL793.B23718   1994
629.4 – dc20   93-33237
                CIP   AC

A number of the illustrations
in this book, which appeared
originally in titles from the
Picture Library, Space Scientist
and First Look series, are based
on material created by David
Jefferis.

Printed in Hong Kong

Series Editor
Norman Barrett

Designed by
K and Co

Photographs by
NASA
Jet Propulsion Laboratory
Johnson Space Center
Aerospatiale
European Space Agency
Lockheed Missiles and
    Space Company
Royal Observatory, Edinburgh

New Illustrations by
Rhoda and Robert Burns

Contents

Comsat

Comsat is short for COMmunications
SATellite. Comsats are used to relay
television, telephone and other signals
around the world. They receive these
signals from ground stations, on earth.
They amplify, or strengthen, them before
sending them to other ground stations.
In this way, TV programs and telephone
calls can be sent all over the world with
no wires needed.

▽ Satellites may be
retrieved in space and
repaired by space
shuttle astronauts. Here,
Dale Gardner locks onto
a stranded Comsat
before maneuvering it
over to the shuttle.

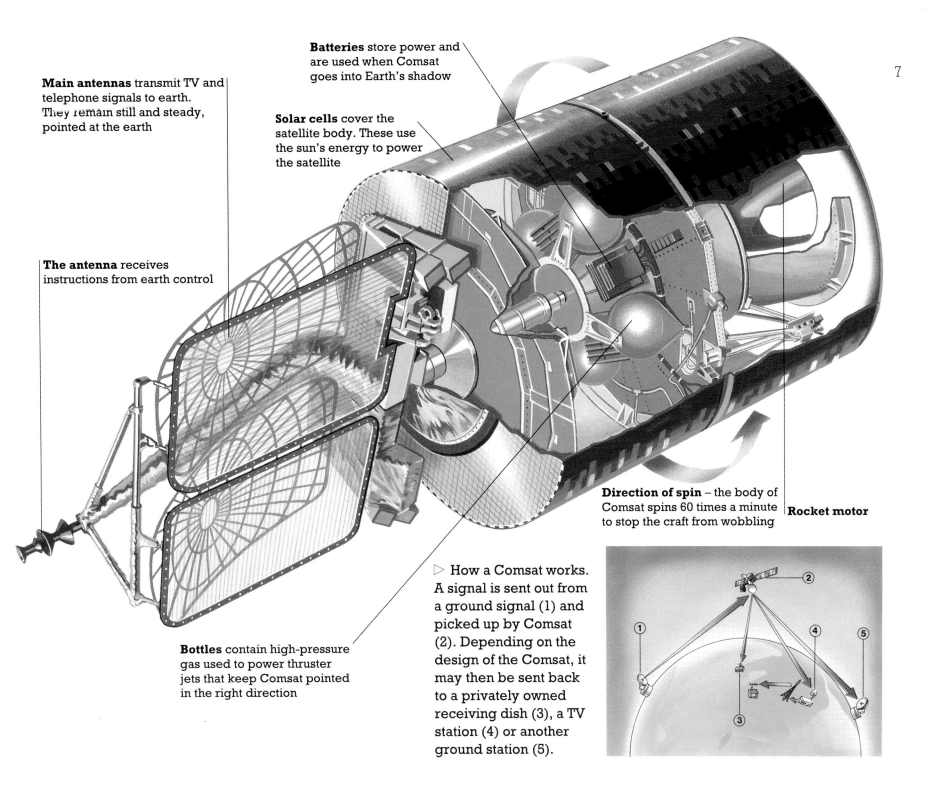

Batteries store power and are used when Comsat goes into Earth's shadow

Main antennas transmit TV and telephone signals to earth. They remain still and steady, pointed at the earth

Solar cells cover the satellite body. These use the sun's energy to power the satellite

The antenna receives instructions from earth control

Bottles contain high-pressure gas used to power thruster jets that keep Comsat pointed in the right direction

Direction of spin – the body of Comsat spins 60 times a minute to stop the craft from wobbling

Rocket motor

▷ How a Comsat works. A signal is sent out from a ground signal (1) and picked up by Comsat (2). Depending on the design of the Comsat, it may then be sent back to a privately owned receiving dish (3), a TV station (4) or another ground station (5).

Other satellites

Thousands of satellites orbit the earth. In addition to Comsats, there are satellites that study the weather, survey the earth, or observe military activity. Some satellites are sent to orbit other planets. Astronomers use satellites and other spacecraft to study the universe.

Many satellites carry radio equipment and a computer. These enable people on the ground to send out instructions and to receive signals in return. The signals are transformed into words, figures, television pictures or sounds.

◁ The French Spot satellite is used to study the resources of the earth. Earth resources satellites, as they are called, use powerful cameras, radars, and other instruments to send back a variety of detailed information. They search for oil and minerals. They map remote areas. They give early warning of forest fires and even the spread of disease among forests and crops.

Solar panel to provide power

Radio antenna

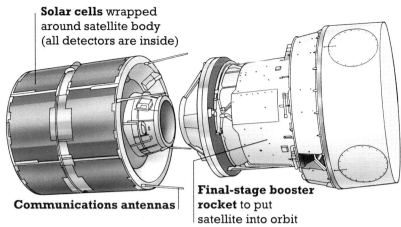

Solar cells wrapped around satellite body (all detectors are inside)

Communications antennas

Final-stage booster rocket to put satellite into orbit

△ Europe's COS-B was the first satellite used by astronomers to study gamma rays from distant stars.

▽ IRAS (Infrared Astronomical Satellite) was the first satellite to study infrared radiation. It made important discoveries in this branch of astronomy.

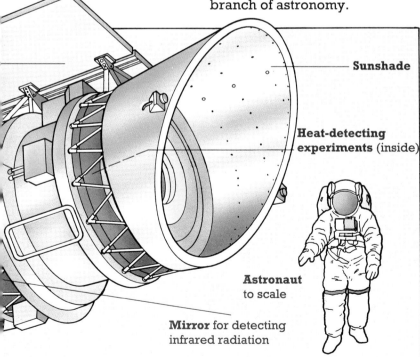

Sunshade

Heat-detecting experiments (inside)

Astronaut to scale

Mirror for detecting infrared radiation

△ The LDEF was a scientific satellite launched in 1984 to study the long-term effects of space on various materials. It was retrieved by a space shuttle in 1990.

▽ Spy satellites are used for military purposes. Some return film in capsules that parachute to earth. Their powerful cameras take detailed pictures of ground installations and activities.

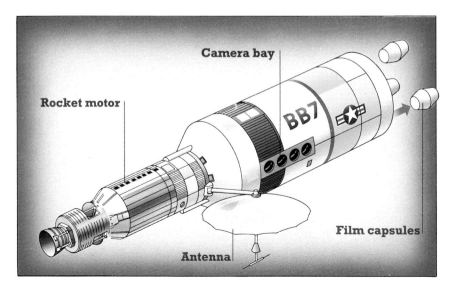

Rocket motor

Camera bay

BB7

Film capsules

Antenna

Apollo

Apollo spacecraft landed the first men on the moon. Apollo carried three astronauts. On missions to the moon, two astronauts landed on the moon in the lunar module, while a third orbited the moon in the command module, waiting to take them back to earth.

In all, there were eighteen Apollo missions, manned or unmanned. Apollo 11 made the first successful moon landing. The next five other missions landed men on the moon, and Apollo 18 made a historic docking with a Soviet Soyuz spacecraft in earth orbit.

◁ American astronaut Buzz Aldrin steps off the lunar lander onto the surface of the moon. The photograph was taken by astronaut Neil Armstrong, the first person to set foot on the moon.

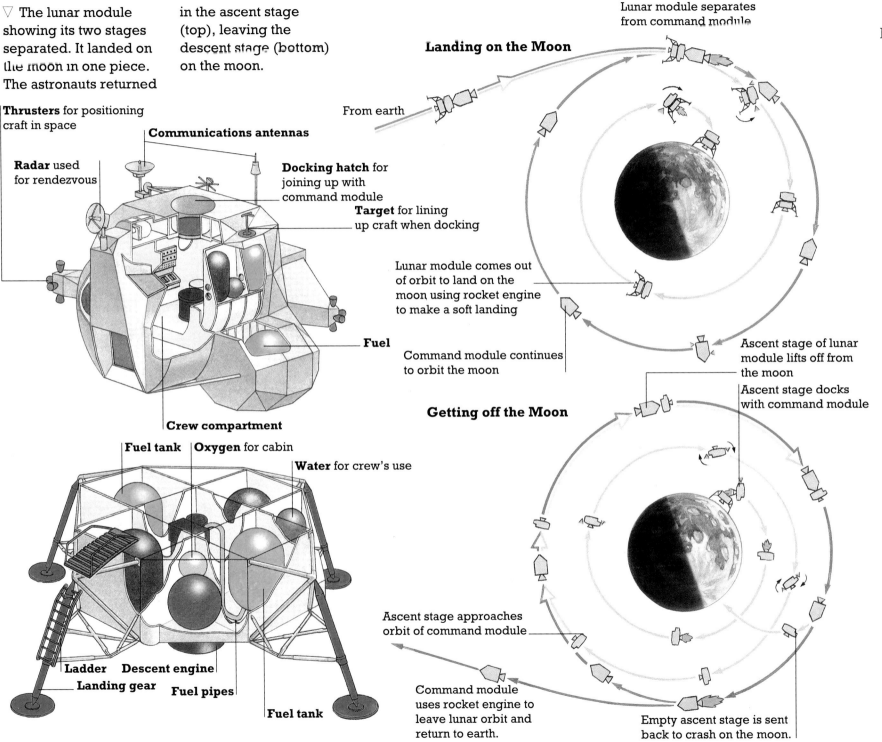

▽ The lunar module showing its two stages separated. It landed on the moon in one piece. The astronauts returned in the ascent stage (top), leaving the descent stage (bottom) on the moon.

Thrusters for positioning craft in space

Communications antennas

Radar used for rendezvous

Docking hatch for joining up with command module

Target for lining up craft when docking

Fuel

Crew compartment

Fuel tank | **Oxygen** for cabin

Water for crew's use

Ladder | **Descent engine**

Landing gear | **Fuel pipes**

Fuel tank

Landing on the Moon

From earth

Lunar module separates from command module

Lunar module comes out of orbit to land on the moon using rocket engine to make a soft landing

Command module continues to orbit the moon

Getting off the Moon

Ascent stage of lunar module lifts off from the moon

Ascent stage docks with command module

Ascent stage approaches orbit of command module

Command module uses rocket engine to leave lunar orbit and return to earth.

Empty ascent stage is sent back to crash on the moon.

◁ The launch of an American space shuttle. The part that goes into space is the orbiter. At the launch, this is dwarfed by the external fuel tank and the two rocket boosters, which separate from the orbiter when their fuel is used up.

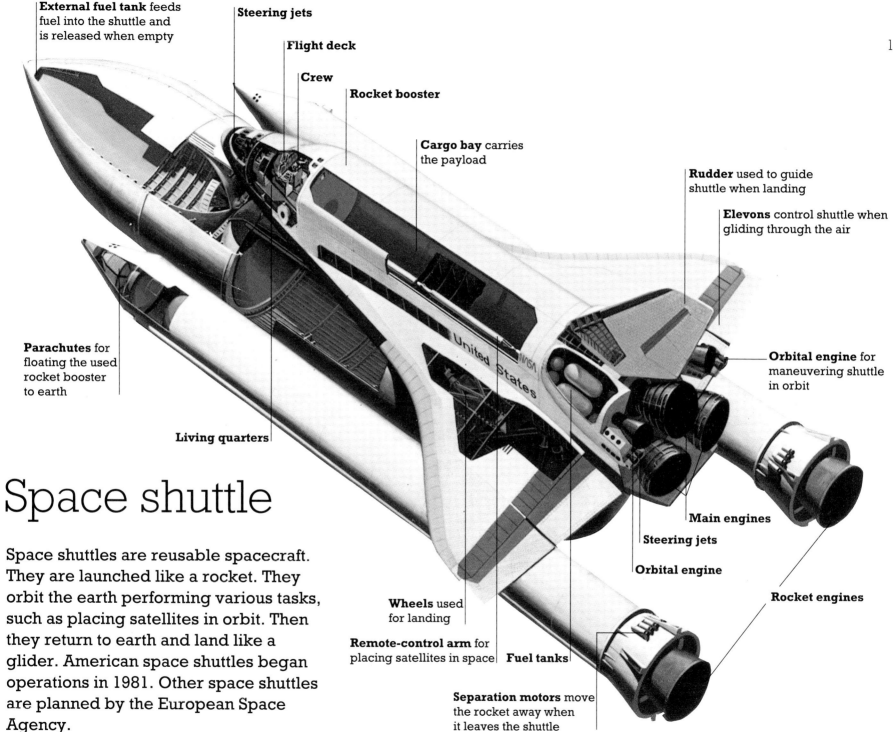

External fuel tank feeds fuel into the shuttle and is released when empty

Steering jets

Flight deck

Crew

Rocket booster

Cargo bay carries the payload

Rudder used to guide shuttle when landing

Elevons control shuttle when gliding through the air

Parachutes for floating the used rocket booster to earth

Orbital engine for maneuvering shuttle in orbit

Living quarters

Main engines

Steering jets

Orbital engine

Rocket engines

Wheels used for landing

Remote-control arm for placing satellites in space

Fuel tanks

Separation motors move the rocket away when it leaves the shuttle

Space shuttle

Space shuttles are reusable spacecraft. They are launched like a rocket. They orbit the earth performing various tasks, such as placing satellites in orbit. Then they return to earth and land like a glider. American space shuttles began operations in 1981. Other space shuttles are planned by the European Space Agency.

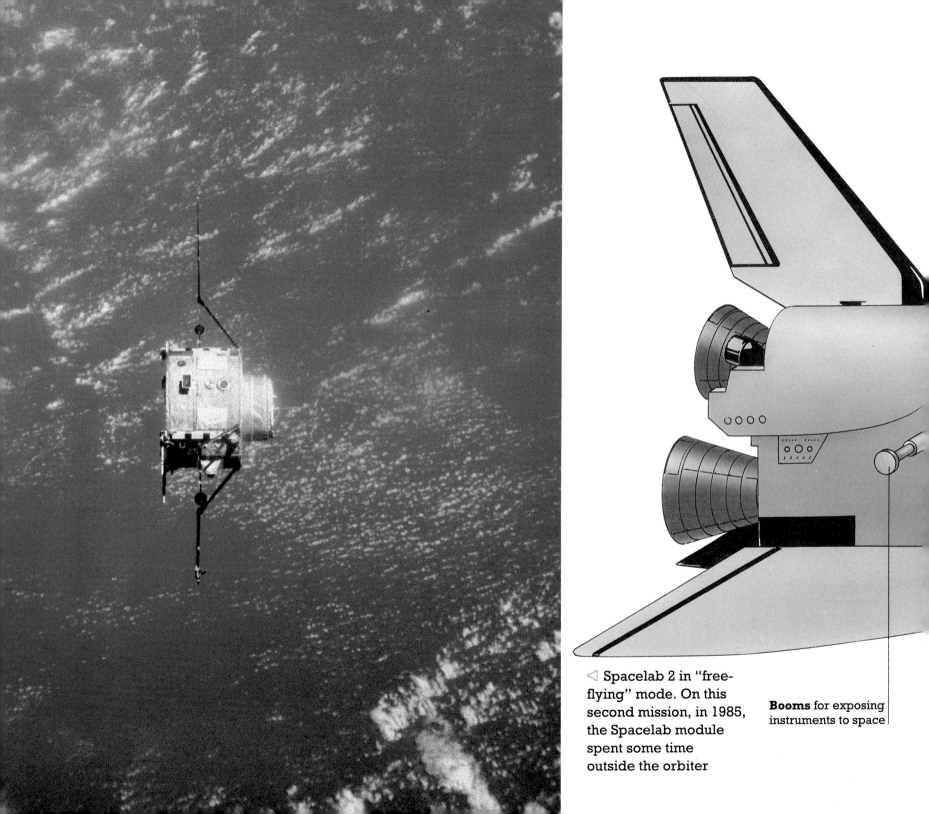

◁ Spacelab 2 in "free-flying" mode. On this second mission, in 1985, the Spacelab module spent some time outside the orbiter

Booms for exposing instruments to space

Spacelab

Spacelab is an orbiting laboratory taken on some space shuttle missions. It consists of one or two modules, in which scientists work, and a number of pallets with experiments that need direct access to space. The modules and pallets normally remain inside the orbiter throughout the mission.

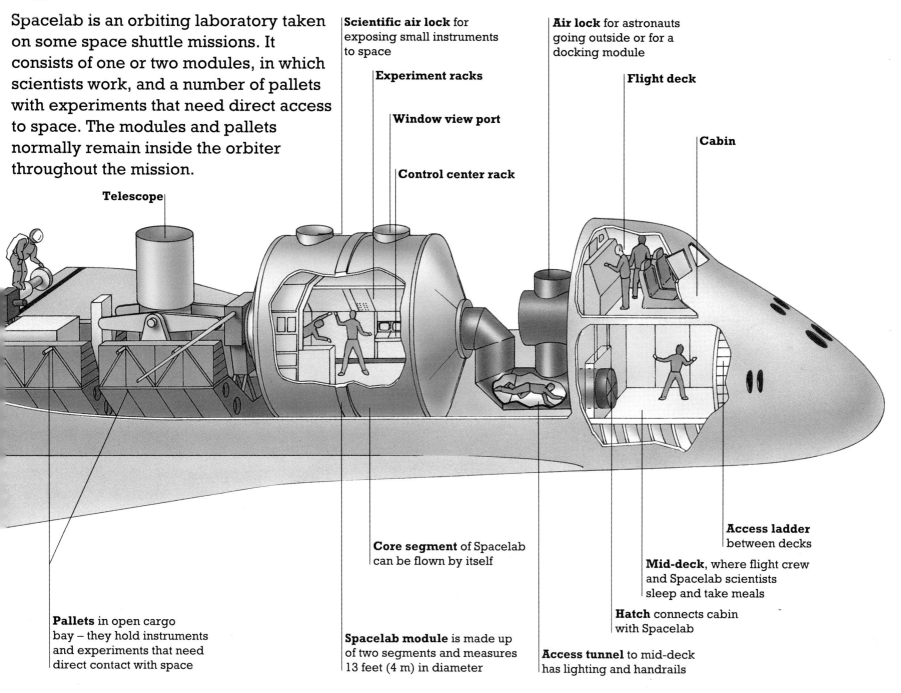

Scientific air lock for exposing small instruments to space

Experiment racks

Window view port

Control center rack

Air lock for astronauts going outside or for a docking module

Flight deck

Cabin

Telescope

Access ladder between decks

Mid-deck, where flight crew and Spacelab scientists sleep and take meals

Hatch connects cabin with Spacelab

Core segment of Spacelab can be flown by itself

Pallets in open cargo bay – they hold instruments and experiments that need direct contact with space

Spacelab module is made up of two segments and measures 13 feet (4 m) in diameter

Access tunnel to mid-deck has lighting and handrails

◁ Using his MMU, an astronaut moves around in space close to his shuttle.

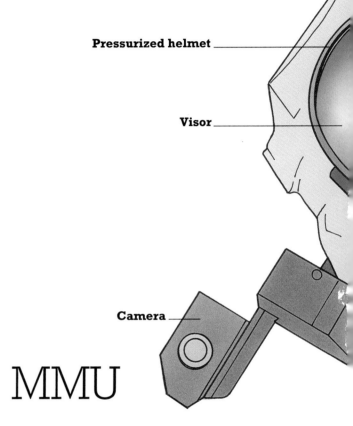

Backpack contains the life-support system. It provides oxygen and keeps the space suit at a fixed temperature

Pressurized helmet _____

Visor _____

Camera _____

MMU

An MMU is a Manned Maneuvering Unit, used by astronauts when moving untethered outside their spacecraft. It snaps onto the astronaut's life-support system.

The astronaut flies this personal spacecraft by operating handgrips on the armrests. These fire gas jets. The astronaut must wear a pressure suit that supplies him with oxygen and keeps his body at an acceptable temperature.

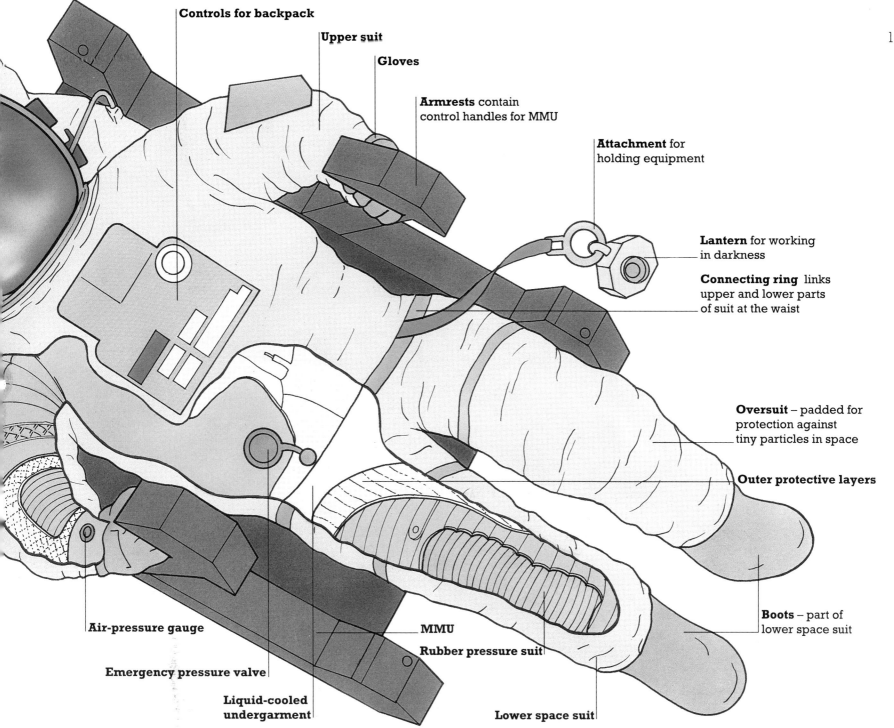

Controls for backpack

Upper suit

Gloves

Armrests contain control handles for MMU

Attachment for holding equipment

Lantern for working in darkness

Connecting ring links upper and lower parts of suit at the waist

Oversuit – padded for protection against tiny particles in space

Outer protective layers

Boots – part of lower space suit

Air-pressure gauge

MMU

Rubber pressure suit

Emergency pressure valve

Liquid-cooled undergarment

Lower space suit

◁ The European space plane Hermes – a project for the late 1990s.

▽ Two minutes after launch, the solid boosters burn out and separate from Hermes. Shortly thereafter, a rocket stage separates, and then the propulsion module. After docking with the Columbus free-flying laboratory and completing its mission, Hermes reenters earth's atmosphere and separates from its resource module, which burns up in the atmosphere. Hermes is then brought down to land like a plane on a runway.

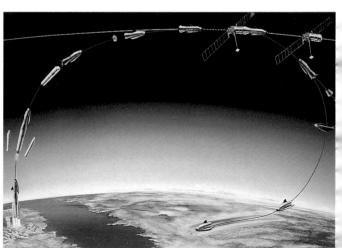

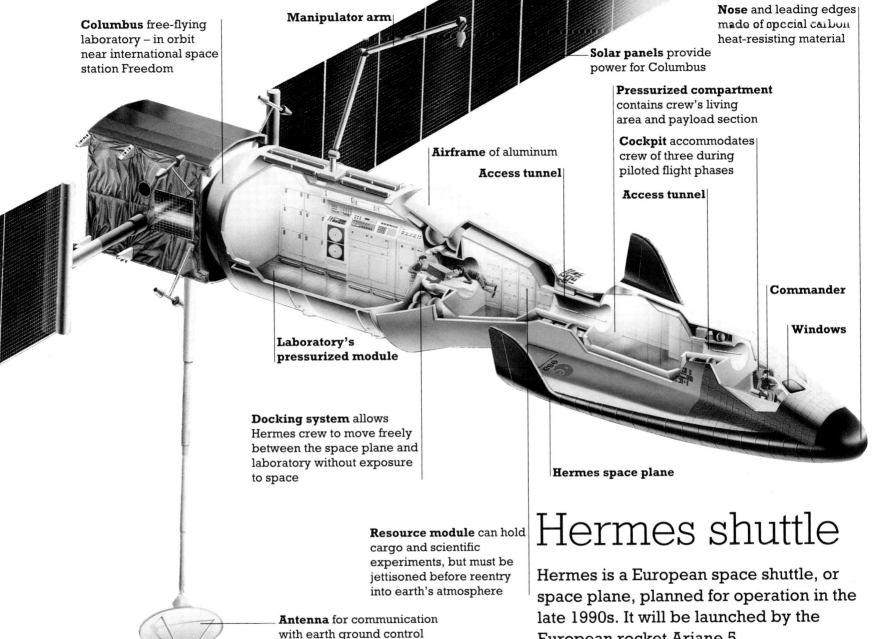

Columbus free-flying laboratory – in orbit near international space station Freedom

Manipulator arm

Nose and leading edges made of special carbon heat-resisting material

Solar panels provide power for Columbus

Pressurized compartment contains crew's living area and payload section

Cockpit accommodates crew of three during piloted flight phases

Airframe of aluminum

Access tunnel

Access tunnel

Commander

Windows

Laboratory's pressurized module

Docking system allows Hermes crew to move freely between the space plane and laboratory without exposure to space

Hermes space plane

Resource module can hold cargo and scientific experiments, but must be jettisoned before reentry into earth's atmosphere

Antenna for communication with earth ground control

Hermes shuttle

Hermes is a European space shuttle, or space plane, planned for operation in the late 1990s. It will be launched by the European rocket Ariane 5.

Hermes' chief mission will be to service the two Columbus laboratories – one attached to the international space station Freedom, the other free-flying close by.

Lunar probes

The Soviet Union and the United States both sent probes to study the moon before the historic Apollo landings. Some probes flew by the moon or went into orbit. Others crashed into the moon or made soft landings. Soviet probes sent back the first pictures of the moon's far side and the first close-ups of the moon's surface

▷ Luna 2 was the first man-made object to reach the moon. A Soviet space probe, it smashed into the lunar surface in September 1959.

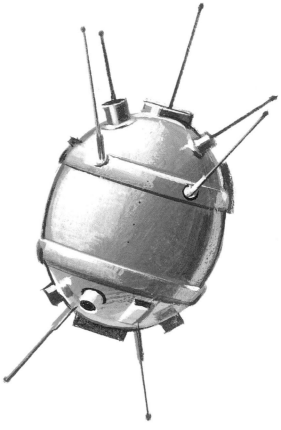

◁ An astronaut on the Apollo 12 mission to the moon in November 1969 inspects Surveyor 3, an unmanned probe that soft-landed on the moon 2½ years earlier.

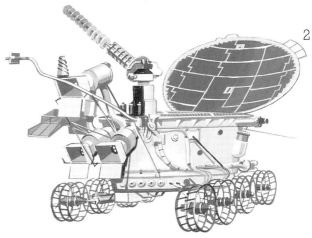

△ The Soviet Lunokhod traveled over the moon by remote control, taking pictures and sending them back to earth.

△ Luna 9 sent back the first pictures from the moon's surface. The spacecraft soft-landed on the moon and ejected an instrument capsule. This rolled over and "petals" opened to reveal a camera and transmitting antennas.

▽ Luna 16 used a drill on a long arm to extract a sample of soil. It was then placed in a container and blasted off back to earth.

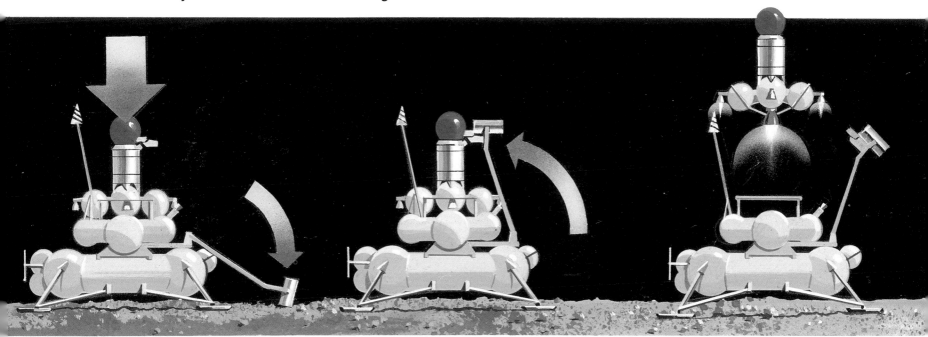

Planetary probes

Spacecraft are sent out to explore the Solar System. These probes orbit or land on planets and their moons. They radio back information and remarkable photographs of other worlds. The first probes were to the moon. Since then probes have flown to most of the planets and some are now on their way out of the Solar System and into interstellar space.

▽ Two probes launched in the early 1970s to study some of the nearer planets. The U.S. probe Mariner 10 (top), launched in 1973, was the first probe to pass two planets. It sent back pictures of both Venus and Mercury. The Soviet probe Mars 3 (bottom) was one of a series sent to study Mars. It reached the red planet in December 1971, but its lander stopped transmitting after only 2 minutes.

◁ An artist's impression of the Galileo space probe orbiting the planet Jupiter, with the moon Io on the left. Sent up by NASA in 1989, Galileo is scheduled to reach Jupiter in 1995.

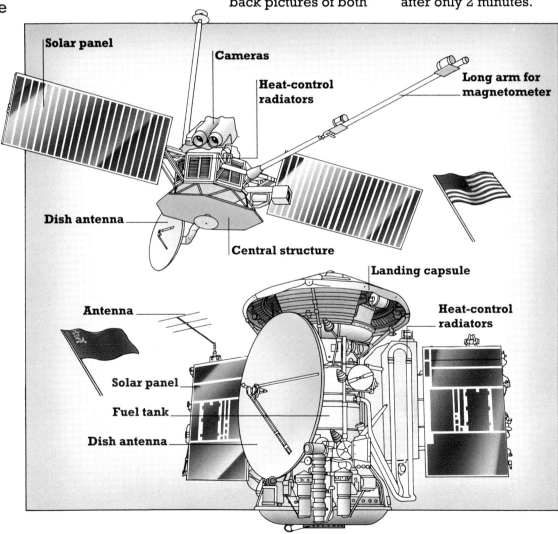

Solar panel

Cameras

Heat-control radiators

Long arm for magnetometer

Dish antenna

Central structure

Landing capsule

Heat-control radiators

Antenna

Solar panel

Fuel tank

Dish antenna

Viking

Viking was the name of two probes sent to study the surface of the planet Mars and to search for signs of life. The two spacecraft carried the same equipment, including two television cameras. They each parachuted a lander successfully to the surface of the planet in 1976 and continued to send back information for several years.

Experiments on the soil of Mars failed to detect any signs of life.

▽ The descent module, or lander, of the U.S. Viking probe, with its soil sampler scoop extended. As well as sending back photographs of the Martian landscape and testing for life, the Viking landers also recorded weather measurements.

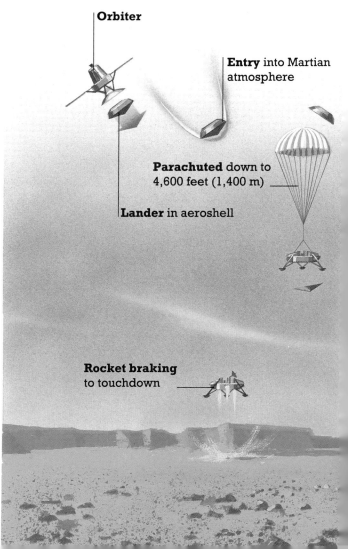

Orbiter

Entry into Martian atmosphere

Parachuted down to 4,600 feet (1,400 m)

Lander in aeroshell

Rocket braking to touchdown

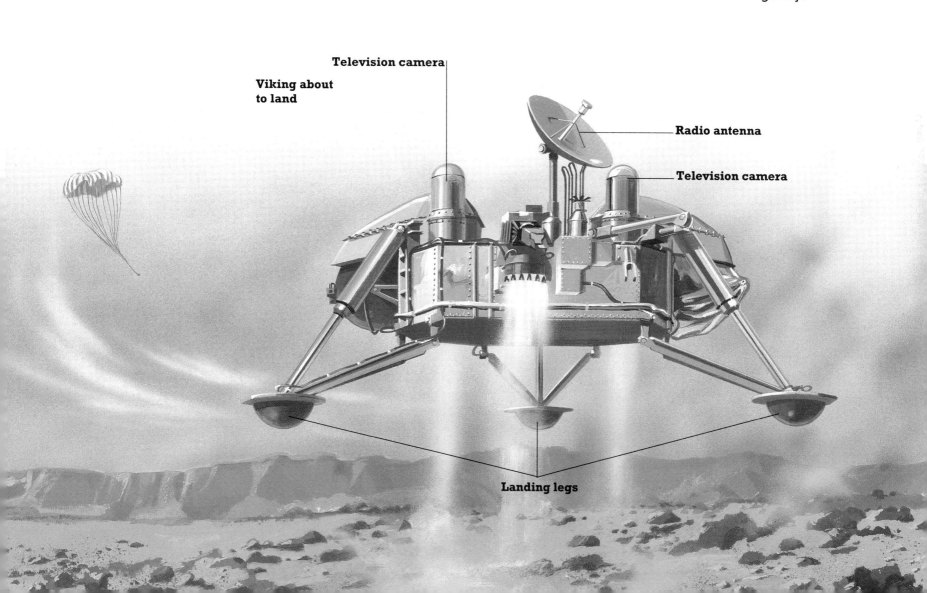

▽ Similar in size to a small car, the Viking lander was released from its orbiter for entry into the thin Martian atmosphere. It parachuted down until close to the surface and then used rockets to land gently.

Television camera

Viking about to land

Radio antenna

Television camera

Landing legs

Voyager

Two Voyager space probes were launched in 1977 to study the distant planets. They sent back wonderful pictures of the planets and their moons before heading out of the Solar System and toward the stars.

The remarkable voyages of these probes were made possible by using the gravity of one planet to "fling" the spacecraft in slingshot fashion toward another. Voyager 2 visited four of the outer planets in twelve years.

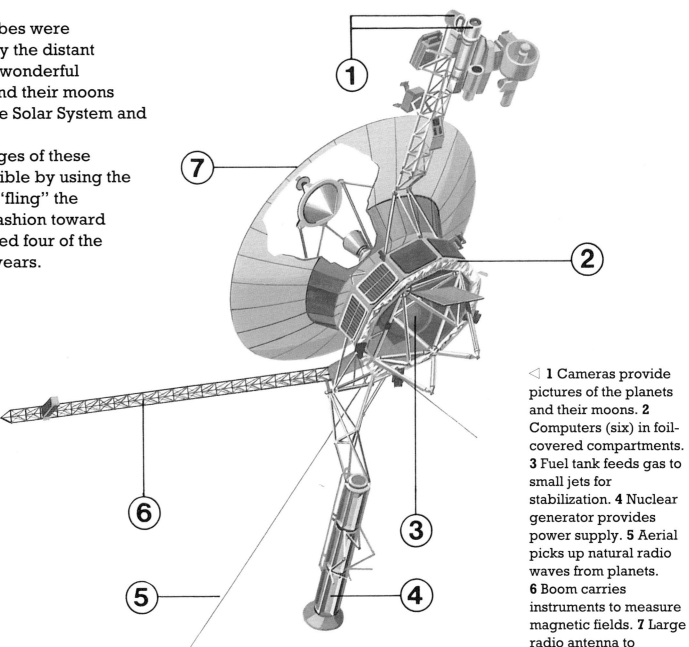

◁ Voyager 2 visited Jupiter in 1979, Saturn (left) in 1981, Uranus in 1986, and Neptune in 1989.

◁ **1** Cameras provide pictures of the planets and their moons. **2** Computers (six) in foil-covered compartments. **3** Fuel tank feeds gas to small jets for stabilization. **4** Nuclear generator provides power supply. **5** Aerial picks up natural radio waves from planets. **6** Boom carries instruments to measure magnetic fields. **7** Large radio antenna to communicate with earth.

◁ The space probe
Giotto on its "suicide"
mission into the coma
(head) of Halley's comet,
which it reached in 1986.
It emerged with some
damage, but was still
sending signals. Other
probes studied the
comet from a distance.

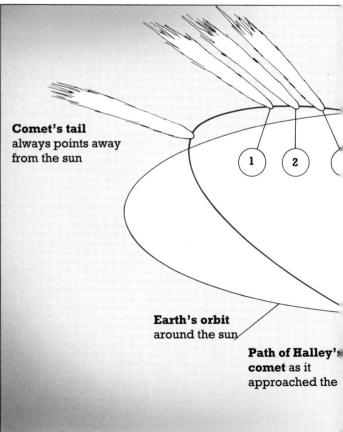

Comet's tail
always points away
from the sun

Earth's orbit
around the sun

**Path of Halley's
comet** as it
approached the

Probes to Halley's comet

Comets look like fuzzy stars when they appear in the night sky. They travel around the sun, sometimes taking hundreds or even thousands of years to make one orbit. They are made up of ice and dust, and glow brightly by reflected light when close to the sun.

In 1985, unmanned space probes were sent out to study the most famous comet of all, Halley's comet, making its first appearance since 1910.

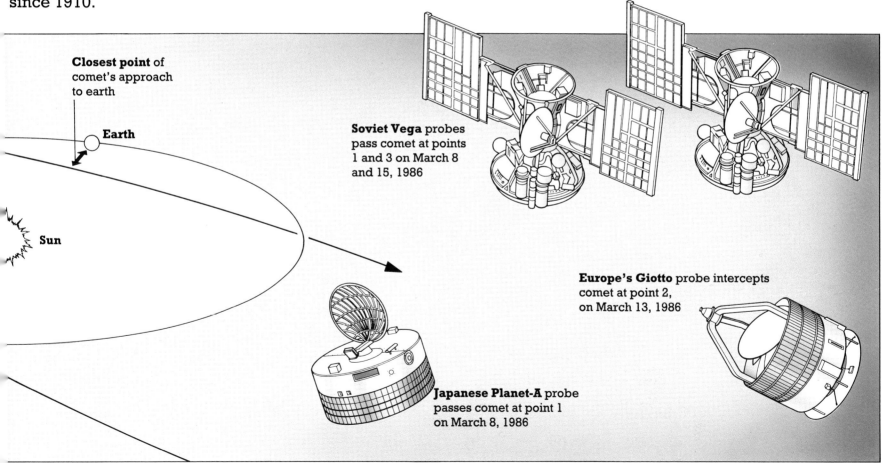

Closest point of comet's approach to earth

Earth

Sun

Soviet Vega probes pass comet at points 1 and 3 on March 8 and 15, 1986

Europe's Giotto probe intercepts comet at point 2, on March 13, 1986

Japanese Planet-A probe passes comet at point 1 on March 8, 1986

Observatory

Astronomers study the heavens with huge telescopes housed in domed buildings called observatories. The dome is opened up at night. The telescope and the opening rotate at the same speed as the earth so that objects may be photographed over long periods. Most observatories are built on mountains, where the air is clear.

▽ The Infrared Telescope, belonging to England, is perched high on a mountain in Hawaii. It picks up only infrared radiation. Other observatories also study radiations invisible to the human eye, such as radio waves or X rays.

▽ Two types of telescopes are used to observe light rays – reflectors and refractors

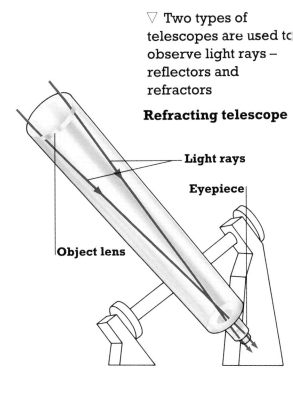

Refracting telescope

Light rays

Eyepiece

Object lens

Reflecting telescope

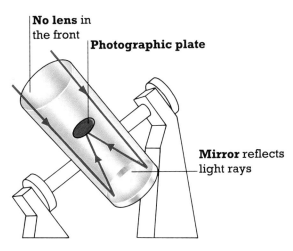

No lens in the front

Photographic plate

Mirror reflects light rays

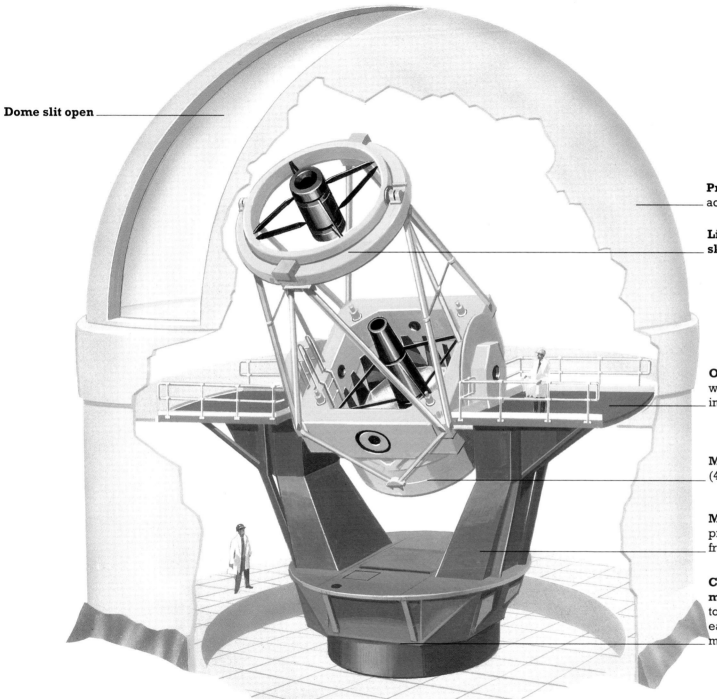

Dome slit open

◁ One of the world's largest reflecting telescopes, the William Herschel Telescope, in the Canary Islands. Most big telescopes are reflectors.

Protective dome acts as windshield

Lightweight skeleton tube

Observation platform, where scientific instruments are placed

Main mirror – 165 inches (4.2 m) in diameter

Massive yoke prevents telescope from vibrating

Computer-driven mounting enables telescope to follow an object as the earth rotates (the dome slit moves at the same time)

Hubble Space Telescope

The Hubble Space Telescope (HST) is an observatory placed into earth orbit by a space shuttle in 1990. Telescopes on earth are hampered by the blurring, churning atmosphere. Space telescopes can see much more of the universe. Distant, fuzzy objects become clearer. Faint objects become brighter. The HST can reach seven times as far into space than the largest telescopes on earth.

◁ The shuttle moves away after placing the 10-ton Hubble Space Telescope in orbit. Despite an unexpected focusing fault in the main mirror, the HST is providing pictures giving 10 times more detail than those available from ground observatories. Astronomers using the HST have made exciting new discoveries.

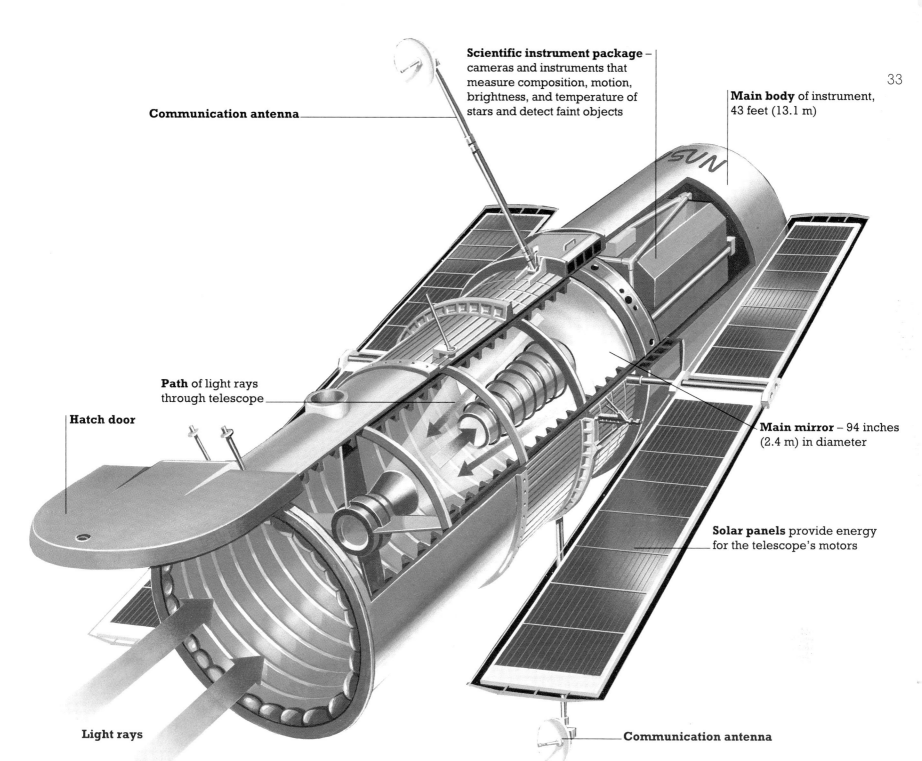

Scientific instrument package – cameras and instruments that measure composition, motion, brightness, and temperature of stars and detect faint objects

Main body of instrument, 43 feet (13.1 m)

Communication antenna

Path of light rays through telescope

Hatch door

Main mirror – 94 inches (2.4 m) in diameter

Solar panels provide energy for the telescope's motors

Light rays

Communication antenna

◁ Astronauts start work on a building project on the moon. This is an illustration from a moon base study carried out by NASA. The idea is to understand the effort required, say, to construct an observatory on the far side of the moon.

▷ How the first moon base might be built. Construction workers unload a module of the lunar base from the spacecraft that landed it on the moon. The module would have been put together at a space station in earth orbit. But once the lunar mines and factories began operating, future parts of the base would be made on the moon.

Moon base

There are plans for the construction of a moon base in the early 2000s. The first crews of four to six might do six-month tours of duty, occupied chiefly with scientific activities. Gradually the "lunarnauts" would expand the base and begin to use lunar resources such as minerals and oxygen extracted from rocks. In time a self-sufficient colony might be set up.

▷ The module is buried under 6 feet (2 m) of loose soil to protect the "lunarnauts" from extreme heat and cold and from bursts of radiation from the sun. Inside the module, they can live and work as they do on earth, except for lower gravity.

Bunks

Work area

Suit storage

Outer airlock

Tunnel to other modules

36

◁ An artist's impression of the international space station Freedom to be built by NASA. It shows a space shuttle about to dock. Space shuttle missions will build and service Freedom, which might serve as a staging post for flights to the moon or Mars.

Docking in space

Docking is the meeting and joining up in space of two spacecraft, one of which might be a space station. The two objects docking are in orbit around the earth or another body and traveling at the same speed, but with proper timing, one may be slowly maneuvered with thruster rockets to join up with the other.

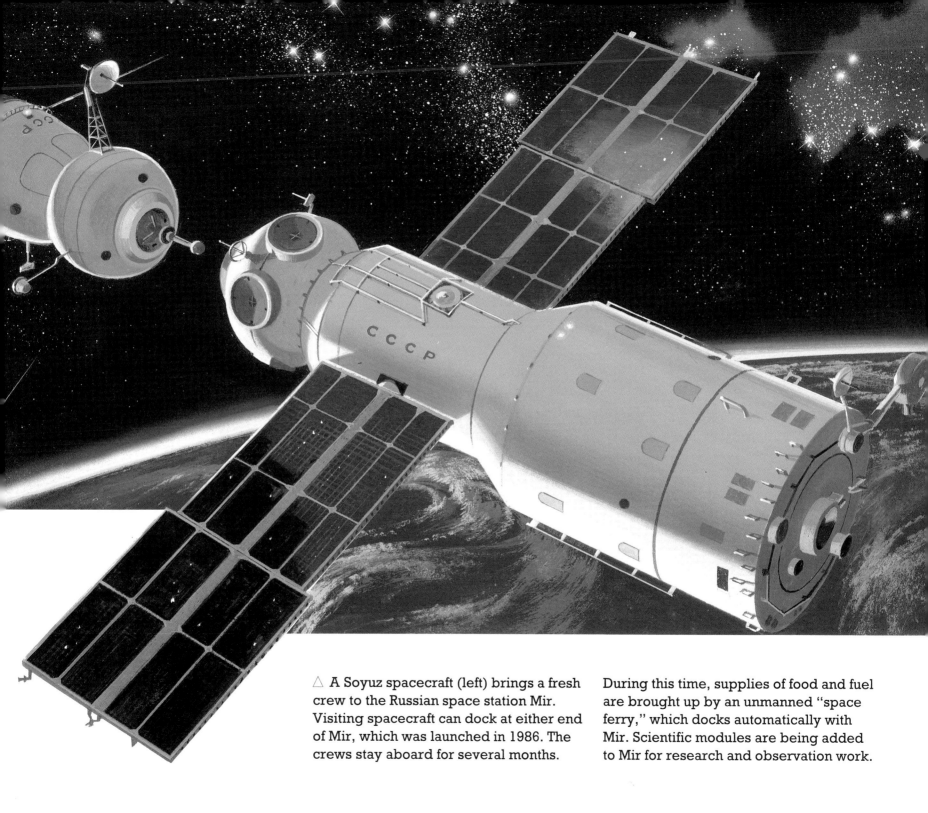

△ A Soyuz spacecraft (left) brings a fresh crew to the Russian space station Mir. Visiting spacecraft can dock at either end of Mir, which was launched in 1986. The crews stay aboard for several months.

During this time, supplies of food and fuel are brought up by an unmanned "space ferry," which docks automatically with Mir. Scientific modules are being added to Mir for research and observation work.

Lunar rover

The lunar rover was a powered vehicle used by astronauts on the last three manned missions to the moon. This "moon jeep," 10.2 feet (3.1 m) long, was landed on the moon folded up like a parcel in a compartment of the descent stage of the lunar module. It was powered by batteries and had a top speed of 8.7 miles per hour (14 km/h).

▽ American astronaut Harrison Schmitt driving the rover past the lunar module on the last moon mission, Apollo 17. The rover enabled astronauts to travel farther from the lunar module than on previous Apollo missions, as much as 4 miles (6.4 km).

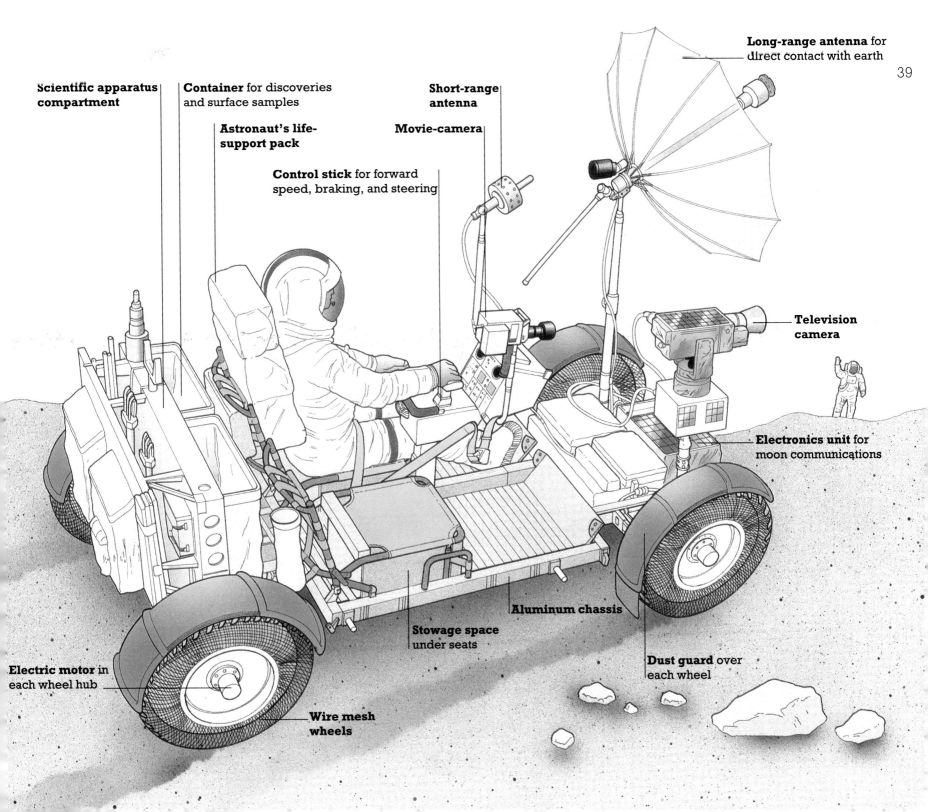

Scientific apparatus compartment

Container for discoveries and surface samples

Astronaut's life-support pack

Control stick for forward speed, braking, and steering

Short-range antenna

Movie-camera

Long-range antenna for direct contact with earth

Television camera

Electronics unit for moon communications

Aluminum chassis

Stowage space under seats

Dust guard over each wheel

Electric motor in each wheel hub

Wire mesh wheels

Future vehicles

Space scientists have been busy designing vehicles for use on future missions to other worlds. The lunar rover used on the last Apollo missions has been developed into a six-wheeled vehicle for extra maneuverability. It will be able to tackle rocky surfaces and steep climbs.

Looking further into the future, astronauts would need special vehicles for operating on places such as the rugged, low-gravity moons of Mars.

▷ Before a manned mission to Mars, a robot vehicle (bottom right) would spend a year collecting soil and rock samples for return to earth. On a possible mission (top right), the mother spacecraft orbits the planet (background) while two astronauts explore the surface of one of its moons. They have landed in a small excursion vehicle (on the ground), and move with the aid of a personal spacecraft.

◁ A six-wheeled roving vehicle on a possible manned lunar mission of the future.

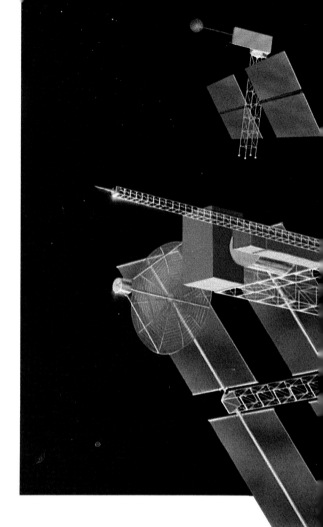

◁ This is what it will be like to work in the international space station Freedom planned by NASA. There are no floors or ceilings in space. Scientists carrying out experiments in zero gravity (relative weightlessness) need to steady themselves on surfaces or rails to avoid floating around.

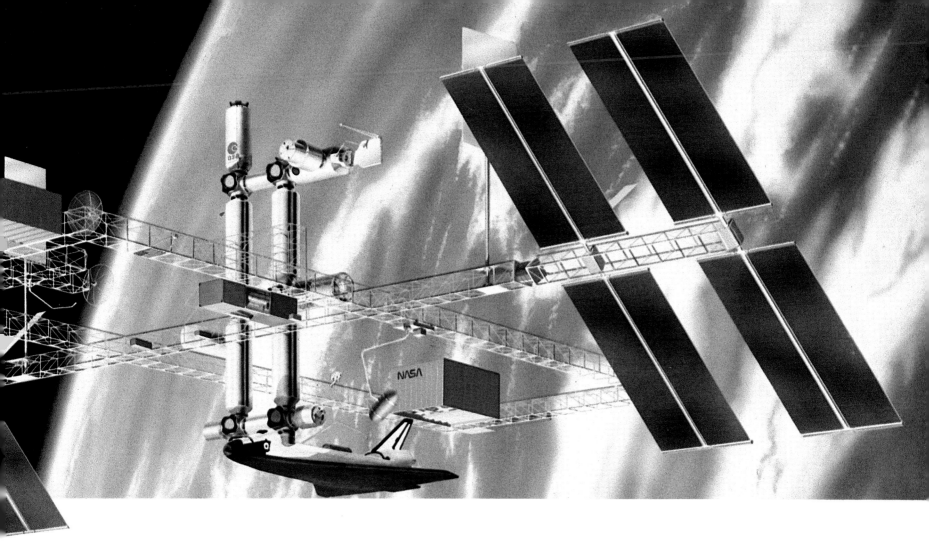

△ A plan for the space station Freedom to be built in the late 1990s by seventeen space shuttle assembly flights. Certain features might have to be reduced in order to cut costs. The U.S. government is funding the operation, but other countries will be able to use the space station. Columbus, the first European orbiting station, will be hooked up to Freedom.

Space station

Space stations are planned to be set up in earth orbit with living and working quarters for space scientists and technicians. As well as being space laboratories, they might also serve as staging posts for manned flights to the moon or Mars. The Russians set up the first permanent space station, Mir, in 1986.

Firsts and fantasies

The first spacecraft

The Space Age began on October 4, 1957, when the Russians launched Sputnik 1, the world's first artificial satellite. Weighing 184 pounds (83.5 kg), Sputnik 1 orbited the earth every 96 minutes and carried a radio bleeper, which transmitted for 21 days.

△ An artist's impression of Pegasus after being launched from a modified B-52 bomber (seen flying off below).

Pegasus, the winged launcher

A new method for launching lightweight satellites into low earth orbit is being developed in the United States. Called Pegasus, it has wings and is launched from a high-flying aircraft. It is then blasted into orbit by a three-stage rocket.

▽ The Magellan spacecraft, sent up in 1989 to orbit and map Venus, was the first interplanetary probe to be launched from a space shuttle. Using radar to penetrate the planet's thick atmosphere, Magellan radios information back to earth.

◁ Sputnik, opened out to show its contents.

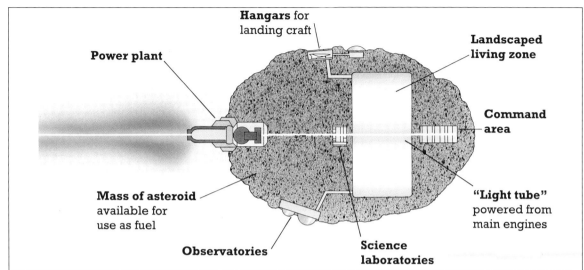

Power plant

Hangars for landing craft

Landscaped living zone

Command area

"Light tube" powered from main engines

Mass of asteroid available for use as fuel

Observatories

Science laboratories

△ In the distant future a "space ark" – hollowed out of an asteroid – could use the gravity of Saturn to swing it away from the sun into deep space. Hundreds of people would live in the ark, and many generations would live and die before it reached a new planetary system they could colonize.

Shooting for the stars

A space shuttle traveling at top speed would take 160,000 years to reach the nearest star. Scientists believe it would be possible to build an unmanned spacecraft sometime next century capable of getting there in 35 years.

> Daedalus, a huge unmanned starship (note space shuttle to scale), designed to blast its way to the stars by a series of nuclear explosions.

Working on other worlds

When people from earth set up bases or colonies on other worlds, there will be much work to do. At first, all their needs will be supplied from earth. But eventually, they will be able to extract essential materials on the spot.

▽ A possible future method for producing energy on another world, like Phobos, a moon of Mars. Astronauts use a mobile nuclear reactor to melt into the surface and generate steam, which is converted into liquid hydrogen and liquid oxygen.

Rocket power

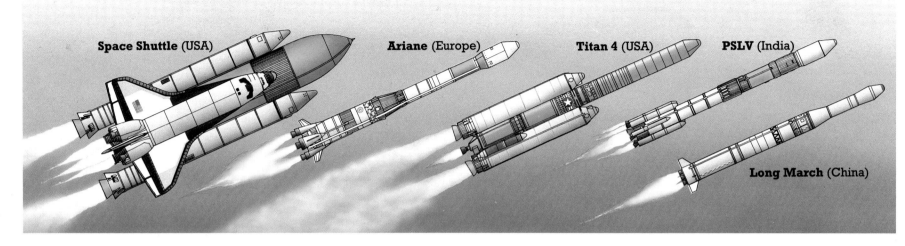

Space Shuttle (USA) Ariane (Europe) Titan 4 (USA) PSLV (India)

Long March (China)

△ The Russians and Americans led the way, and now several countries have rockets capable of placing satellites or other spacecraft into space. Space shuttles may be used many times over, but ordinary rockets are used just once.

▽ A Soviet Energia rocket with their space shuttle, Buran. Energia is the world's most powerful rocket. It can lift payloads weighing as much as 90 tons (100 t) into space.

Rocketing into space

Without rockets there would be no Space Age. All the satellites, probes and other spacecraft that have traveled into space from earth have been put there by rocket power. Other means are being considered for use in space travel, such as nuclear explosions, but in the near future rockets will continue to rule.

Rockets work by burning fuel to make gases. These rush out of the bottom of the rocket and send it off at great speed in the other direction. It is like untying the neck of a balloon and letting it go – the escaping air sends it flying off. A nozzle at the bottom of the rocket helps to control its direction.

More power

The greater the weight of a rocket and its payload, the more power is needed to launch it into space. With multistage rockets, the weight is reduced as each stage drops off.

▽ Rockets are transported to the launchpad by special vehicles. This is the Soviet Molniya.

△ A Titan-Centaur rocket launches the Voyager 1 probe on its historic journey to the outer planets.

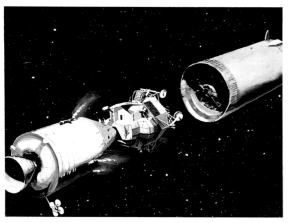

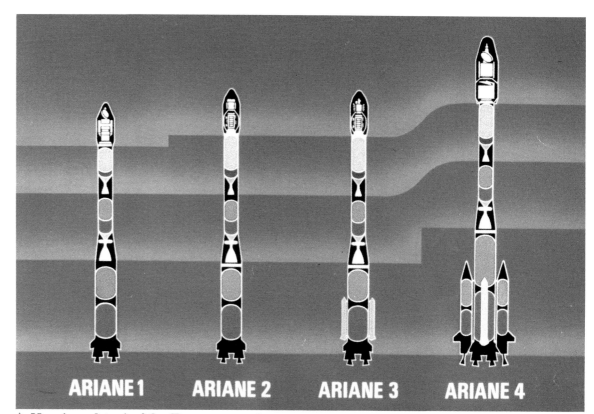

ARIANE 1   ARIANE 2   ARIANE 3   ARIANE 4

△ Versions 1 to 4 of the European rocket Ariane show the gradual development of a rocket as more power is needed. Ariane 4, the latest and most powerful version, can launch payloads of more than 3½ tons (4 t) into space. A more powerful version, Ariane 5, is planned for the mid-1990s, capable of lifting 17 tons (19 t) into space.

◁ An illustration showing how an Apollo spacecraft separated from the last stage (left) of its rocket on the way to landing on the moon.

▷ The first launch of an Ariane 4 rocket, in June 1988. It put three satellites in space.

Index